THE NEW MOM'S GUIDE TO

Dealing
with Dad

THE NEW MOM'S GUIDE TO

Dealing
with Dad

Susan Besze Wallace
with Monica Reed, MD

Revell

a division of Baker Publishing Group
Grand Rapids, Michigan

© 2009 by MOPS International

Published by Revell
a division of Baker Publishing Group
P.O. Box 6287, Grand Rapids, MI 49516-6287
www.revellbooks.com

Printed in the United States of America

Library of Congress Cataloging-in-Publication Data
Wallace, Susan Besze, 1969–
   The new mom's guide to dealing with dad / Susan Besze Wallace with Monica Reed.
     p. cm. (The new mom's guides ; bk. 3)
   ISBN 978-0-8007-3300-1 (pbk.)
   1. Mothers—Psychology. 2. Mothers—Family relationships. 3. Fathers. 4. Father and infant. 5. Mother and infant. I. Reed, Monica, M.D. II. Title.
HQ759.W312 2009
646.78—dc22
                             2008040176

The information provided herein should not be construed as prescribed health-care advice or instruction. The information is provided with the understanding that the publisher does not enter into a health-care practitioner/patient relationship with its readers. Readers who rely on information in this publication to replace the advice of health-care professionals, or who fail to consult with health-care professionals, assume all risks of such conduct.

Published in association with the literary agency of Alive Communications, Inc., 7680 Goddard Street, Suite 200, Colorado Springs, CO 80920.

Contents

Introduction

Joining Forces

It was just a few hours. They're fine. He's the dad, after all.

My husband's first time alone with our newborn was about to end. I'd been to a friend's baby shower, my first outing after having our first son, and I couldn't wait to get home. I felt oddly tied to the little guy, as if I'd been cast out like a fishing bobber to float around in my sleep-deprived state, and the strong bond already established between my son and me was relentlessly reeling me back home.

He needs me. I think they need me. They must need me. I am the mom, after all, keeper of the milk and all sage decisions about this baby's every moment.

When I walk in, the house is quiet and a bit messy. They are lying together on a blanket in the living room, exchanging adoring looks. I think I butted in. I think I'm jealous.

It seems my loving husband had taken our six-week-old to the library, gotten him his own library card, and checked out a few books. It was ridiculous and utterly admirable.

"It was so fun to do something that was his first," Todd said. "Everything he does is a first, but it's usually with you."

That simple outing was the inaugural run of the adventurous, why-not, could-be-fun, let's-learn-something attitude my husband has brought to every day of parenting since then.

He does things his way, and I think I've finally learned to let him.

Nothing enriches a marriage—or stretches it—like the addition of a child. Mom's fatigue and a crying baby wreak havoc with your sex life. Babies are expensive. Date night requires the help of a third party if you want the date to go anywhere. The household chores are harder to get done, and delegating might be a new concept. Mom and dad each have their own style of parenting, both eager to be successful and appreciated.

A new life also brings daily joy and the opportunity to share it with the person you love most in the world.

Several of the baby books I devoured began by extolling the importance of putting your marriage first. Usually I skimmed that section. *I'm already married*, I thought. That part was "done." I was in search of the how-tos for producing an amazing and manageable child.

Well guess what? All babies are amazing. Manageability is an attitude, not a goal. And the books were right. Loving your mate—giving him top priority—gives your child a secure start in this world. Both of you are learning to dance when neither of you knows the steps. Occasionally you will step on each other's toes. But the tango of trust and the waltz of what-ifs were never so rewarding.

Asking for Directions

Directions

Letting Dad Find His Rhythm

From the moment my husband began changing our baby's first diaper in the hospital, I knew parenting was going to be an exercise in learning how to keep my mouth shut. He was loud—joyful but loud—as the baby cried, and he went through wipe after wipe after wipe, trying to scrape that tarlike meconium poop off our little boy. He dropped the diaper, and the bassinet started to roll away. It was a hysterical scene that his parents watched, laughing and doing little to help, except hand him those seventeen wipes. I could tell they loved what they were seeing: their son and his son on the first of many adventures.

They enjoyed being spectators, but they would be nearby if my husband ever needed them.

It was a great lesson for me, who, had I been able to get out of bed, would have been suggesting, instructing, and generally trying to take over the whole procedure.

Dads have to find their own rhythm and start bonding with baby on their terms. Looking back, I should have been thrilled that my husband was so excited about changing a diaper instead of worrying about his technique. Some dads aren't comfortable with their miniature, helpless newborn, and they leave the baby stage to mom. What a shame! Even while still in the womb, a baby knows dad's voice and is ready to connect that sound to a strong set of arms and a comforting scent.

When my third son spent seven weeks in the neonatal intensive care unit, the nurses encouraged moms and dads alike to lay their tiny newborn on their bare skin. Those valuable minutes we

"At the end of the day, who cares if the diaper isn't on **exactly right?** Let the man of the family **make his mistakes.** I think the most **fun** comes from making some mistakes and **figuring it out.** And it's also important from a **bonding** standpoint. I had Taylor for three days once, and I let him play through one of his naps. He didn't go down for like an eternity. It was crazy. He was so tired he couldn't sleep. I learned that lesson better because **I learned it; I wasn't handed it."**

Brandon

had with A.J. changed the way I looked at bonding and daddy time. It was limited, and most often Todd and I went separately to cradle that two-pound boy and all his tubes. I was experiencing what most dads do on a daily basis with a healthy newborn at home: a limited window in which to forge a connection with someone you aren't sure knows you are there. Like many dads, in those early weeks, I struggled with the feeling that my baby seemed more like a project than a person.

Moms have to facilitate the connection between dad and baby. We must try to make that window of opportunity bigger, and not stand, nose against the glass, judging his every move.

I know a man with a very loving wife, who has been known to stick her hand out like a crossing guard holding a stop sign when he's attempting to help. It drives that dad batty. Most men are trusted with decisions of great consequence at work, but at home they can be repeatedly second-guessed.

Maybe your hand isn't out, but do your words halt your husband's efforts to parent?

My friend Tracy said life with a newborn was far from the ideal picture she had developed in her mind. Her world felt rocked, but her husband's seemed to be business as usual.

"I contributed to that," she said. "I made him feel the baby could do nothing without me. I'd leave them together and come back and say, 'You didn't feed him at three? That's going to mess up my whole day.'

"I'd criticize what outfit he picked, how he fed him, how tight the diaper was. I just wanted to do it right. I wanted everything to run smoothly, and mistakenly I thought he ruined that every time I left."

Tracy's husband eventually let her know she might as well take the baby with her if she was always going to come home frustrated about how he did things. So she finally relaxed, realizing that

"I remember the day our third daughter was born, my husband brought the other two girls to the hospital in half-pajamas and half-clothes.

He thought they went together. They had Fourth of July ribbons in their hair.

It was December!

It was all wrong. But I thought,

Why do I care?

They're here and they are happier than they'd be if I dressed them perfectly. I want them to have the greatest relationship with their dad, and to trust him. And they do."

Tania

doing things differently didn't mean doing things wrong.

Mom, decide what really matters. I've never known a dad who didn't at some point pick an outfit for a child that made mom's jaw drop in disbelief. Somehow they can always find the one shirt with the stain or the pants you put in a storage tub because they had become high-waters. But if the child is safe and comfortable, who really cares? If it means that much to you, let your husband know gently without tearing down his efforts. Actually I think my husband enjoys seeing my reactions to the wild wardrobe combinations he picks out—or allows our boys to choose. But finally I've discovered that there are much more important things to worry about than a kid wearing mismatched socks or sleeping in his play clothes.

Some things, of course, are nonnegotiable. If you see your husband feeding popcorn to your eight-month-old, you must say something—hopefully without losing your cool. Maybe tear out that baby magazine article on choking hazards and ask him to take a look. You'd hope for the same caring-not-condemning approach from a friend, wouldn't you?

Sleep, discipline, and safety are the things my husband and I have decided we must approach in the same way. What are your nonnegotiables? Ask yourself, *Is this a one-time daddy-is-doing-it-his-way moment, or is it working against a healthy habit I'm trying to establish?* (We're still debating whether it's a safety issue when dad thinks it's not cold enough for a hat and jacket and mom does.)

Sleep is a biggie, and in our house we say you must "respect the nap." That means when it would be really fun to run by Home Depot, you don't do it if you know your child is ten minutes from naptime—even if she seems pleasant enough at the moment. As you grow as a parent, and your baby hopefully grows into a flexible child, you can decide when to push her and if you can afford the consequences. But early on, respect the nap.

Some dads like to learn things on their own. It's the old resistance to asking-for-directions syndrome. They prefer their one-on-one time with a child to be governed by serendipity, and they will resist attempts to program it. That will be hard for you to accept if you are the kind of mom who lays out clothes and a packed diaper bag the night before you make a fifteen-minute trip to the grocery store. But you must let dad be dad.

Some fathers may be eager for you to share that article on bonding or that flier on daddy story time at the library. They want some direction and suggestions but not a three-color PowerPoint on how they should spend time without mommy in the room. Ask your husband how you can help him find his groove as a parent and expand his comfort zone. Ask him to let you know when it's more help-

"My husband was recently dusting off a fan, and I didn't even realize I had stopped to watch. Without even turning around my husband said to our son, 'Mommy likes to watch me do things to make sure I do it right.' Ouch!"

Vanessa

ful for you to back off. Don't set him up to fail by watching him drive away, knowing he forgot the baby's bottle. That's just mean—and not good for your baby. He'll meet up with plenty of trial-and-error moments all on his own, just like you will.

Deep in the heart of every parent is an aching desire to do this job well. To hear the words "You're a great mom" is like being handed a glass of lemonade on a scorching summer day. It's refreshing and it keeps you going. I don't know why it's hard to remember that dads need affirmation as well. Maybe it's because they seem so capable and strong in other arenas. We seem to have no problem pointing out what they aren't doing or what they could do differently, but what about the gifts they bring to fathering—those things that make you glad he's their dad?

One friend's first child spit up more than he kept down. She found burping him very frustrating and one night, in a moment of hopelessness, turned him over to her husband. It turned out that he had the magic touch.

"I am so glad I let him try," she said. "Otherwise I would have never known."

Another friend's husband would sit with their baby on his lap and play video games, which really got under her skin. "I finally decided to talk to him about it. I didn't realize he wasn't just playing video games. He was telling him all about sports, explaining who his favorite players were and why, and bonding with him in a huge way," she said. "Granted the baby was five months old, but they were bonding. He didn't need to be cooing at him to connect."

My husband swaddled far better than I did, creating perfect little burritos out of his baby boys and their blankets. He is still able to sing a crying child into submission and infuse his boys with a wide-eyed sense of possibility. It began when he held them as babies and told them about

"I think the biggest mistake couples make is around expectations. We put a lot on our husbands and set the bar very high. One year I decided to let my husband take care of the Christmas stockings. He got the biggest kick out of going to Wal-Mart, but he bought absolute junk. Nothing sugar free. Nothing educational. I was horrified. But the kids played with the stuff in their stockings more than their major presents. He also started the tradition of hiding their stockings. What a hit! I said, 'It's yours, always.' You have to let them parent in a way that's natural to them."

Denise

famous military battles. He's always been a grand storyteller.

Tell your husband what you treasure about his fathering. Ask him what he thinks his strengths are.

Finally, find humor in each other's missteps, and tuck away memories of your goofs. My mom recalls a day she left us home alone with my dad, and he simply forgot to feed us lunch. Just forgot!

My friend Jenn told me she and her husband were so sleep deprived that one night he put their baby back in bed without a diaper. Kristi remembers her beloved dressing the baby in a snap-up onesie—putting her arms where legs go and her legs where arms go. Write these things down! They are the patches of the quilt that is your parenting. Each square makes you stronger and wiser and contributes to the bigger pattern of love and grace you are trying to create together.

Dealing with Dad
Looking Inward

1. What can I do to encourage a strong dad-and-baby bond?

2. How do I feel when my husband does something differently than I would?

3. Am I prone to instructing my husband rather than just letting dad be dad?

Riding
Shotgun

Strapping Yourselves Together

When relatives are in town, and we out-number the seat belts in the car, my family occasionally does something we like to call "the double buckle." Two people click themselves together in the same seat belt, usually overlapping each other and often sucking in their collective gut for a short ride. It's not the safest and takes closeness and personal hygiene to a whole new level.

The last time I double-buckled it happened to be with my husband. (Don't worry; he wasn't driv-ing.) Once I remembered that thankfully, yes, I had just brushed my teeth, I got a little thrill from being in his lap. It struck me how long it had been since

I'd been there. In college, piling in and cozying up were the norm. As newlyweds and for years after, I'd crawl into his lap spontaneously.

With a new baby, there is quite literally something that comes between a husband and wife. Stick with me here, and move away from thinking about highway safety.

As parents, it's crucial that you double-buckle. You must stay close physically and emotionally and face the bumps as a team. Overlap your hands and your hearts as often as possible. Remember those days of electric proximity and hang on to each other.

In a car you'd never put a baby between you and your husband in one seat belt. They have their own straps and buckles. It's the same in everyday life. You are responsible for your children's well-being, but that doesn't mean they have to be front and center all the time. The primary safeguard of their life is your marriage.

Putting your marriage first might seem automatic and logical to you. It didn't always to me. We tried for years to have kids, and I assumed that when they finally arrived we were to give them our everything. That's what makes you a good parent, right? Protect them at all costs, scrutinize everything from the brand of diapers to their academic development, decide what they should do and when and with whom, read to them daily. My responsibility screamed to me: kids first! What I should have heard is: kids always!

Growing up is a marathon, not a sprint. New parents need to calm the sense of urgency they have about doing everything for their kids—doing everything right and doing it all right now—to see that their long-term strategy for parenting is what matters.

The most important piece of your parenting strategy is maintaining a strong marriage. Harmony between mom and dad injects a household

"My parents didn't just kiss.
My parents made out
in front of us.
I have to say that felt really awesome.
I can remember the feeling it brought
to me to know that they were
in love.
That's really important
to who I am today."

Hillary

with stability. It nourishes the emotional development of a child. Remember how you felt when your parents argued? Because parents are their kids' world, their arguing colored everything and may have scared you. When our kids' world begins to quake, we can't underestimate the snaking cracks that form in their emotional foundation and stick around long after the quaking has stopped.

Yes, arguing is normal and will likely happen your entire marriage. It can even be healthy for kids to see, depending on how you resolve conflict. But even though it's normal and you resolve conflicts quickly, it still affects your kids, and only you and your spouse know how much quaking there is going on.

Also it's important to keep in mind that it's not just what your children see you do in your marriage that impacts them, but what they *don't* see you do. Do you hold hands? Do you greet each other? Do you forgive? Do you trust? Do you laugh? If you are emotionally blank with one another, they learn from that too.

Kids, of course, make life busier. You've probably already started the routine of "You get the diaper bag, and I'll get the baby." That can develop into "You take him to football practice, and I'll stay home to nap the little guys." Soon you are dividing and conquering every time you go anywhere—out of necessity. I liken it to a football team. Different coaches handle different aspects of different players, but when it's game time, a united front is crucial. Be mindful of staying a husband-wife team whenever you can for the tone it sets for your family.

By integrating children into your life, not plopping them at the top of the family totem pole, you accomplish several things. You are establishing emotional security. You are also modeling marriage and male-female dynamics, and what a huge responsibility that is! Often I think of the parents

"Your marriage is like a
beautiful garden.
If you don't take care of it,

it will grow full of weeds,

no matter what great plants

you started out with."

Denise

out there molding my future daughters-in-law. The idea that my little men will love another woman someday is tough to think about! I pray for these little girls to become generous, nurturing women because of what they see in their parents.

One day all our children will leave the nest. If they leave a nest that has been completely transformed to fit their every whim and wish, they are in for a rude awakening. The world will not cater to them that way. Certainly the comfort and happiness of our kids should be important to us, but there's far more to parenting than "padding" the world for them. I want to raise servant-hearted, appreciative little people, not kids who think the world owes them something.

Another thought: when it's empty nest time, you don't want to be left to share the rest of your life with a stranger. It happens every day to couples who have so focused their lives on their children that they have forgotten the reason they chose their spouse in the first place. It's incumbent on you to stay linked with your partner in a very real way.

Dealing with Dad
Looking Inward

1. How are my husband and I setting priorities in our marriage?

2. What gifts does each of us bring to parenting? How are we supporting each other as we find our groove?

3. What's changed most for us as a couple since having a baby? What are our biggest challenges?

Table for Two

Ideas for Staying Connected

We're a goal-oriented society. Meet someone, check. Introduce him to the folks, check. Engagement, check. Marriage, check. Thrive in career, check. Get pregnant, check. Have baby, check, check, check, check, check.

The milestones in our babies' lives are spelled out. They learn to eat, to walk, to talk. Formula and diaper companies send mail on coping with each stage, just as your child approaches it. Then they go to school and are promoted grade after grade after grade.

Marriage is different. This precious, life-giving relationship—one that statistics show has to fight to stay alive—doesn't come with guidelines or graduations. What's the last marital "check" you had? The last time I was told what to do as a married person was when, on my first anniversary, I was supposed to eat frozen wedding cake. No advice has ever come in the mail on keeping marriage from getting stale.

It seems easy enough with a newborn. They sleep a lot, and even though parents are tired from the twenty-four-hour cycle of caring for a new life, they have time to catch up and focus on each other. That is, if they can talk about something besides their new addition.

Make no mistake, a newborn baby should be a blessed new center of attention. Every movement is mesmerizing, every feeding a great adventure, and every day holds new things to experience and accomplish. But as baby grows, something starts to happen quietly and gradually—and to the best of parents. Kids get more demanding and more vocal. They require more of your heart, your pantry, and ultimately, your marriage.

"We had good jobs, made decent money, and hung out. It was one giant date. We played all the time. How did we not know that was ending? We thought adding a baby would just add to our current life, not create a new one. It's a good life, but it's very, very different."

Liz

When Todd and I were young marrieds living in California, we thought nothing of seeing two movies in the same day, or even driving an hour to Hollywood to see one, just because we could. That's four hours of sitting next to each other, not counting the leisurely lunch and drive time we had in between. The thought boggles my mind as we now have to carve out minutes just to finish sentences to each other. During a rare recent trip to the movies, we actually ate a take-out dinner we snuck into the theater. Time was limited, and, well, we really wanted to see a movie. How's that for staying connected?

Date night is certainly one way to stay close. Look forward to those evenings. Leave notes for each other that say, "Can't wait to hold your hand!" Plan *together* what you'll do. Newborns sleep in fairly predictable stints, which makes an ice cream outing with the stroller very doable. If you can leave the baby, a date doesn't have to be long, just an hour for

"We went into ourselves a little when we first had Sam. For me it was identity; for my husband it was exhaustion. We communicated, but it wasn't about who we were. We were just trying to figure it out. Now we debrief after the kids are in bed. We have a glass of wine and we talk about everything— friendships, work problems. We're always on the same page because we do it just about every day. If we start debriefing just about the kids, we make ourselves stop and go back to you-and-me."

Angela

Retreat
and Renew
THE MARRIAGE WEEKEND

My sisters and I gave my parents a "marriage enrichment" weekend as a Christmas gift when I was in college. It wasn't so much that they needed relationship help as it was that we thought they deserved the chance to get away.

Quite frankly, it was all the vacation we could afford to give them, but we knew they wouldn't want to spend even that much money on themselves.

That weekend, which was offered through their church, prompted my mom and dad to start a regular date night. They were asked to return to future marriage enrichment weekends as facilitators, and they found they had a passion for working with engaged couples. Today they are employed in family ministry, working daily with couples who are beginning their married life or looking to save it.

You never know what seeds such a retreat will sow.

"Why wouldn't you take the chance to get to know even more the one you love?" my mom says. "Even after forty years there's still room to become closer, find more joy, experience more satisfaction from marriage."

While I have to say running into people who have heard my parents give "the sex talk" at a marriage or engaged couples retreat is a little unnerving, I couldn't be prouder that they make their marriage a priority and have spent years helping to fortify hundreds more.

Attending a marriage weekend doesn't mean your relationship is in trouble, just that you want to nurture it. Many churches require preparation courses for engaged couples, but isn't it funny how once you're "in," it's up to you?

Your local church is the best source for finding local marriage retreats. Also the Weekend to Remember network of marriage conferences can be accessed at familylife.com or 1-800-FL-TODAY (358-6329). Learn about Catholic Worldwide Marriage Encounter weekends at www.wwme.org or 909-863-9963.

"I was so ready, so excited to become a parent that it became the *focus*. Now that my kids aren't babies needing constant attention—and they like playing at the neighbor's house as much as ours— I'm starting to look at my main *relationship* again, and it's not the same as it was before kids. My role as a father is changing, and I'm realizing my *marriage* has too. We went to Mexico for our tenth anniversary and took the kids because I feel like I never get to see them. In retrospect it would have been much more a relationship builder to go by ourselves. I wonder if I feared not having them there because for so long it hasn't been *just us*."

Reuben

coffee or a walk. The important thing is to regain and retain the habit of focusing on each other.

You don't even have to leave the house. Rent a classic DVD for a buck and eat popcorn. Play poker. Cook a late dinner together and eat under the stars or picnic in the living room. Creativity can be more memorable than cash when it comes to a date. Your goal here is to look into your spouse's eyes and relate. To talk about what's affecting your days and your heart. And to hear the same from him.

Try getting physical. For now I'm talking about exercise. Walking or hiking together, swinging the tennis racquet, or swimming at the local recreation center will do your mind, body, and marriage good. Google "date your husband" on the Internet and there'll be almost no end to the ideas and inspiration for dates from friends and books. Ask around, or check out *Date Night in a Minivan* by Lorilee Craker. You'll soon come up with your own best idea, just from getting the romantic juices flowing.

On the
ROAD AGAIN

Having a husband who travels for work is a fact of life for many women. Thousands of men serve in the military, and they are gone for long chunks of time. That's particularly wearing on a new mom. Not only is her best friend gone, but so is her sleep relief, a second set of arms, and the person she wants most to share baby's milestones. Here are a few ideas on staying connected and easing the separation.

Before...

- Beware of "premature detachment." That's when you know he's going to leave and you withdraw because you think it will make saying good-bye easier. You jump in the foxhole and steel yourself for going solo—but he's still around. If you need to prepare, talk about it. But you don't want to be aloof and cause an argument that will linger in the air as he leaves.

- Put current photos in his briefcase or suitcase. Write baby's size on the back in case he finds a cute souvenir while he's gone.

- Plant his favorite snack for him to find during his trip.

During . . .

- Talk every day if you can, but realize you might be in different time zones or certainly on different schedules.

- Resist the temptation to replay every detail of your day. Create a box in which you can put notes on the kids' notable accomplishments ("Our baby girl started responding to music today!"), so you can remember to share them when he has time to fully appreciate the news.

- Establish boundaries for both of you when it comes to spending time with co-workers or friends of the opposite sex.

- If travel is the norm for your spouse, look at it as just that—normal. Don't think of travel as something he does to the family, but something he does for the family.

- You are busy, but think what a nice surprise getting a love note would be while he's on the road. Express your appreciation for his daddy efforts.

- Don't shop away the time. Spending money might feel good in the short term, but it could add to your stress in the long run.

- Give yourself something to look forward to while he's gone. Watch a good movie.

- Have a friend over for dessert one night after baby goes to bed. Ask a family member or a friend to help you have a few hours to yourself.

After . . .

- Hopefully you've created systems that work while dad's been gone. But don't make him feel like an outsider when he returns. Be especially careful not to criticize his care of the kids when he's getting his feet on the ground again.

- Plan some couple-only time if possible, but expect that he might be torn between spending time with you and the kids.

- Reconnect physically. Don't punish him for being gone by distancing yourself.

Solve the babysitting problem. Money is often an issue for a young family, and therefore babysitting can be too. Try swapping children with another couple you trust. They get two or three child-free hours, and then you do. You can do this the same day or alternate weekends. Usually, leaving baby with an adult is easier for new parents than hiring a teenager to babysit. With your mind free from concerns for your child and the cost of her care, you are free to listen to and enjoy your mate.

This brings up a good point. Try not to dump on your spouse every baby detail and emotion that have crossed your heart and mind in the past month. On your date allow him time to talk too. Let him share the latest from work. Ask questions.

Engage in an activity or go to a place that will remind you that you are people not just parents.

Staying connected won't happen by just wishing it so. It's also unproductive to whine that your husband isn't planning the fun. You can set the tone.

Tell him how important it is to you. Schedule it. Write it down. And have a backup plan if a sitter backs out.

Also, be flexible about your expectations. Recently, one Friday morning, my husband told me to pack a bag. I had a mighty full day, and the former me would have been flustered at the lack of notice. But I just went with it, *so* grateful he recognized the need for us to be just us. We were going to spend the night at a historic downtown hotel—even better, at a discounted rate. We had to adjust our plans several times to get the kids situated with his parents, get dinner without a long wait, and generally get in our heads there was no right or wrong way to spend our time. It was a wonderful twenty hours of just being us.

You cannot expect one evening to erase all stress, restore all sleep, facilitate every conversation, or answer every question. But one evening at a time, reconnecting will help you build a marital foundation that will withstand the pressures and distractions of raising a family.

Dealing with Dad
Looking Inward

1. How are my husband and I doing at staying connected as a couple?

2. What appeals to each of us as an activity or opportunity to help us stay close?

3. What are the obstacles to our spending time alone together? Have we really tried to find solutions to them?

Wanted

Diaper-Changing Mind Reader
Able to Function on Little Sleep

"He doesn't automatically know you are exhausted and moody. You have to tell him."

Elizabeth

It's not that I was keeping score, but there was just something about being awake, alone, feeding that first baby, the exhaustion so deep it was nauseating. I'd walk back into our bedroom with a big sigh, maybe flush the toilet unnecessarily. And I'd surely not go to any trouble to slip back in bed quietly. *Huff, huff, flop, roll, siiiiigh.*

Sometimes my husband heard; sometimes he kept right on sleeping that hard, deep, enviable sleep.

Recently my mother shared with me that she did the same thing with my dad.

"One of my clearest memories is pounding the arms of the rocking chair because I felt so alone," she said. "I was frustrated because he was sleeping and I wasn't. But I didn't know how to tell him."

Forty years later women are still trying to communicate at 3 a.m. without words. When will we learn?

New moms and dads face a very steep learning curve, especially when it comes to expressing themselves. Sleep deprivation makes us edgy and volatile. Uncertainty about what baby needs at a given moment can make us defensive. Hormonal shifts make mom prone to communicating with tears, a language that often baffles dad. Moms and dads can both suffer postpartum blues and even depression. Often in women this means overt sadness, whereas in men it can manifest itself in irritability and hostility. When you're both feeling

Fighting Fair

- Drop the "gun language," as it's called when you wag your finger like a firearm and point out "you this" or "you that." Stick to "I" statements.

- Avoid personal attacks and name-calling. Remember the tremendous power your tongue has to wound or uplift your spouse.

- Don't lose control. Arguments should never be abusive and should never be so explosive that you aren't able to stay beyond your kids' earshot.

- Don't say, "You always" or "You never." Stick to the issue at hand.

- The longer an argument goes, the uglier it can get. Set a time limit. If you don't know when it's over, you probably don't know what you want to accomplish. Figuring that out first can save a lot of hurt.

- Don't make a mountain out of a molehill. Also, just because you could get mad about something doesn't mean you have to.

- Remember, one of you shouldn't emerge the winner. The relationship should.

so much that defies words, feelings may remain unexpressed until they explode.

Communication is crucial between new parents. Every day a mom thinks about a gazillion things and makes about as many decisions. She has a nonstop conversation with herself. But it's easy to forget that hubby isn't privy to all those thoughts. He doesn't know this is the fifth time the baby has started to cry and the fifth time you haven't been sure why. He may see that your hair is in a ponytail, but that doesn't mean he knows you are feeling down and unfeminine because you haven't had the time to shower. He may see a full laundry basket (or two or three), but he may not know how important it is to you to get something finished in a day.

Likewise, when *you* see a well-dressed guy come home from life in the grown-up world, you may not know that he spent the day worried about providing for you and his new child on one income.

Mom goes nonstop each day; most likely she's the primary caretaker and, well, she *is* the mom. It's easy for dad to take for granted that she's doing okay—tired but okay. This is what women do, right? His mom did it, and yours did too. But you are probably facing an incredible learning curve every day with your baby. You have doubts. You still need to be taken care of, but you can't expect your husband to read your mind. Sure it would be nice for him to just *know* when you need a cozy robe, a pep talk, and a giant bowl of mocha almond fudge ice cream. We all want to be understood that way.

Help him.

You have to tell him what's going on, or he won't know what you're thinking. And you need to tell him with careful attention to what you say, when you say it, and the tone of voice you say it with.

My friend Vanessa said that as much as she and her husband planned for their first baby, sleep

"Somewhere in that first year,
I longed to be a *child* again.
I wanted someone to
put me down for a nap,
to anticipate my needs.
I wanted to be sick just so
someone would care for me."

Noell

deprivation and quarreling caught them off guard. "We never really argued before then. Now it was about things that didn't even have to do with baby, like making the bed right. I don't even think we realized it was the lack of sleep making us so edgy until he was about two years old.

"I never agreed with 'don't go to bed angry.' We would have never slept because we were always arguing about something."

You are tired and possibly overwhelmed as a new mom. That's not a permission slip to be ornery, but it is encouragement that you're not alone in letting your tongue slip now and then. Sometimes, as sleep deprivation creates a little paranoia, couples can make their new-baby-era quarreling into something it's not. It's likely, though, that your marriage isn't crumbling, just being reshaped by parenthood.

My husband said that as his patience with our children grew, his patience with me diminished somewhat. Unfortunately the same happened for

ROCKY ROAD:

If you were experiencing difficulty in your marriage before having a baby, those problems might be exacerbated by the new responsibilities a little life brings. How do you know if your marriage needs outside help?

All marriages face challenges and even crises, but persistent hostility, the absence of communication, withdrawal, and real or contemplated infidelity are just some of the signs that your most precious relationship could be in jeopardy.

Consult a professional counselor or a pastor trained in marriage counseling if you're not making progress on your own. Respect the privacy of your relationship—even when it's frustrating you—and avoid sharing details with other family members or friends. *This never means, however, that you should endure abuse.*

"I tried for years to change him. I knew it was wrong. My parents' marriage wasn't like that," Stephanie remembered. "But I didn't know what to do about it. I'd always have to wait and see which of his moods showed up. It wasn't until I worked on me that I could see the truth. It was like a light went on inside me: *God hates divorce, but he also hates you being abused.*"

If something about your relationship with your partner

scares you and you need to talk, call the National Domestic Violence Hotline (NDVH) at 1-800-799-SAFE (7233).

According to the NDVH, you may be in an emotionally abusive relationship if your partner calls you names, insults you, or continually criticizes you; does not trust you and acts jealous or possessive; tries to isolate you from family or friends; monitors where you go, whom you call, and with whom you spend time; does not want you to work; controls finances or refuses to share money; punishes you by withholding affection; expects you to ask permission; threatens to hurt you, the children, your family, or your pets; or humiliates you in any way.

You may be in a physically abusive relationship if your partner has ever damaged property when angry (thrown objects, punched walls, kicked doors, etc.); pushed, slapped, bitten, kicked, or choked you; abandoned you in a dangerous or unfamiliar place; scared you by driving recklessly; used a weapon to threaten or hurt you; forced you to leave your home, trapped you in your home, or kept you from leaving; prevented you from calling police or seeking medical attention; hurt your children; or used physical force in sexual situations.

Taking care of yourself is more important than it's ever been. You have a child depending on you.

"During the first six months if not more after your child is born, it's a good rule that what is said past a certain hour—1 or 2 a.m.—is forgotten. I think it's easy to compete for a *solution* and it's easy to misinterpret each other. It's hard to keep an open mind and take that step back when the going gets a little tough. But you have to know when you've said enough and when to walk away."

Brandon

me. I just wish I'd realized what was happening years ago. Some days you muster every ounce of serenity and staying power for the little one, and there's just little left for the one you married. Daily I pray for more patience with my husband and for everyone in my life, including myself.

When you do fire up a feud, agree to revisit disagreements *after* a night's sleep, and you might not even remember what you were arguing about. I know this flies in the face of "don't go to bed angry." I'm not saying go to bed angry; just go to bed. A good night's sleep is often the best medication any couple could ask for. When you do put an issue to rest—and ladies, you know I'm talking to you here—let it truly rest.

Finally, avoid the cheap shots that come from communicating *through* your child: "Well, Daddy really loves football, so I'm going to stop what I'm doing to change your diaper so he can keep watching the game, okay?" Sound silly? Harmlessly sarcastic? Maybe, but you never want to involve your children in your disagreements. Start now making that a line not to cross.

Dealing with Dad
Looking Inward

1. How are my husband and I getting along since the baby was born? What do we attribute this to?

2. When is the best time for us to communicate?

3. In the middle of the night when I'm up with the baby, I feel . . .

4. Something that's been on my heart that I've kept to myself is . . .

5

Lobbying for Hobbies

Finding Peace in What's
His, Mine, and Ours

My mom was in a Yahtzee group with some other young moms when we were very little. I didn't know until recently that it was so important to her that she kept her dice date one night even though her parents were arriving from out of town.

"It was *my* night," she said. "That's how important it was."

My dad was and still is a huge fishing aficionado. It might as well have been written in their vows that he would love, honor, and cherish a boat and any chance he could get to sit on a quiet lake and reel 'em in. Those weekend tournaments began to look a little different to my mom when she was

"I think it's hard for a new mom to conceive of keeping up a hobby, and it's hard for her to watch her husband spend time with his. We tend to keep score, noting the number of days or hours 'off' each one has. But you don't get anywhere by giving your spouse a guilt trip. Men get time away because they take it. I think women are waiting for someone to give them permission. You have to communicate what you need. I know the last thing you want is to say it, but men need to hear it."

Brandon

left home alone with three little girls. She felt just that—left alone.

Hobbies take on a new dimension when maintaining them means leaving your partner with the children. And affording your pastimes now means weighing personal pleasure against the expense of raising a family. Before hobbies become a source of resentment, new parents would be wise to communicate and negotiate with each other about the hobbies they love.

Some moms feel conflicted about expressing their personal desires, let alone satisfying them. They feel—and rightly so in some situations—that they should deny themselves for the good of the children. Dads are less circuitous in their thoughts. If they want to go golfing or attend a poker night, they say so.

You raise an eyebrow. You're tired. You imagine hours spent alone with the baby. Those thoughts stir up some guilt. You realize he worked all week, but you did too. You both want the weekend to feel like a weekend, relaxing and fun. But there's a third party to consider now.

We women tend to overanalyze, and sometimes men underanalyze. Whichever way you lean, think compromise. That's different from tallying hour-for-hour who gets to do what. See the opportunity to give your spouse some time as an opportunity to love him better. Don't play games. Tell him if you miss a pastime you used to find fulfilling, or that it's particularly challenging to spend big chunks of time alone with the baby on a Saturday afternoon. Talk about how you can work together on these things *before* they become the subject of an argument.

Remember whom you fell in love with. It's likely that a hobby, or at least how your husband approached his joys in life, was part of what attracted you to him in the first place.

My friend Barb became a mom at forty-one. She was fearful that because she had to wait longer

"Before kids, we understood that as long as we worked hard, we should be able to enjoy our passions. After kids, I didn't understand why I couldn't still go out in the woods for a week of hunting or fishing without a major guilt trip when I returned. It was my not wanting to own up to my newfound responsibilities as a father, and I took it out on my wife. It got to the point where I dreaded going hunting or fishing because I feared the repercussions when I got back. This made me resentful, and that made things worse. Instead of understanding where she was coming from, all I cared about was how I needed to make myself happy. Ten years of marriage and three kids later, we have learned to compromise regarding my hobbies. I am so thankful for my wife and her understanding of me and of pastimes that are as much a part of me as my hands and feet."

Chris

than most for motherhood, her son could become all-consuming—unhealthy for him and for her marriage. When baby was one month old, Barb was intentional about attending a women's retreat.

"I knew I had to do it then to set a precedent," she said. "I had to take the plunge. It surprised some people—I got a look or two—but it went really well. I think sometimes moms aren't sure of what's 'right' so they don't look out for themselves."

Moms and dads need to have their personal niches, but it's also important to find something to share besides the kids. For now, it might be a Friday night movie at home, not mountain biking or seeing Europe. It doesn't matter what you do, as long as you do it together. Parenting can send couples in different directions, and that gets even more intense with multiple kids and their many activities. Invest in sharing things now so that time together is a reflex, not a rare experience.

"Don't begrudge something
your spouse is
passionate about.
Love is letting the other person
find him- or herself too."

Mary

I don't enjoy running, and my husband wouldn't touch a scrapbook page if you paid him. But while sharing passions isn't always possible, sharing what they mean to you is. I understand that pushing himself physically makes my husband a happier guy. It's not about running *away* from us. In the same way, he understands that cropping is a way for me to process where I've been as a mom and that it feeds my need to create, journal, and finish things. I like the outcome of his running. And he likes the outcome of my scrapbooking. So we give each other space and respect for these things whenever we can realistically.

Realistic is the operative word. You can't do it all when you have small children. You have to accept that some things will take a backseat for a while. And this may be frustrating. But for me, it would be far more frustrating to want kids and not be able to have them. So, gratefully, I embrace this season and know that likely, in the next, I will be able to do more of the things that give me personal fulfillment.

And I embrace my husband, without trying to hold him hostage from doing the things he enjoys.

Dealing with Dad
Looking Inward

1. Before my husband and I had children, what activities inspired us? What did we love about them?

2. Do we "keep score," noting the time each of us spends on personal pursuits away from the family? Are we both getting what we need?

3. What activity could we share during this season of early parenting?

Overstuffed

The Dollars and Sense
of Providing

ach day, when I was pregnant with my first son, I'd slide open the closet door in the nursery and caress his little clothes. Some were baby shower gifts, but many were things I couldn't resist buying for him. You want to *do* something for the child you're expecting. I couldn't hold my unborn son, but I sure could buy him a wardrobe.

When he was little, I continued to collect his "stuff." We spent time cruising the mall, and I continued accumulating. I couldn't yet teach him his ABCs, but I could get him that adorable jacket on sale or the toy I was sure would be a big hit.

Oh to have some of that money back now! I don't regret providing for my children, but how

I wish someone had told me how little a child really needs. I wish I had known how fast we'd start drowning in toys—and how much would be handed back and forth between family and friends that we—I—didn't need to buy.

Studies show that money is the number one source of marital strife. Usually that strife is the result of couples leaving their expectations for how they will live and how they will spend unspoken.

"Beginning or expanding a family doesn't bring on new financial issues as much as it amplifies any and all of the financial issues the parents were already facing," said Jordan Jackson, a presenter with the Good $ense ministry. "I would strongly encourage new parents to use the experience of having a child as a great motivator to implement good financial basics. . . . Resist the cultural message that you and your kids deserve to have it all right now."

Preparing for the
Unthinkable

What will happen to your child if something happens to you and your husband? It's a stomach-churning topic but a necessary one. You can draw up a will and have it notarized, or you can consult an attorney to write a will for you. And be sure your loved ones, especially those who will be affected by it, know it exists.

With your husband, answer the following questions when deciding the potential guardianship of your children:

- What are our values in raising our child? What are our thoughts on education and our religious convictions? Who is best suited to follow through on our wishes?

- Who already has a good relationship with our child?

- Where do they live?

- How old and how healthy are they?

- Do they have children? How would the couple's children affect the future of our child?

- How would this couple feel about being named our child's guardian?

- How do finances come into play? Would raising our child be a strain?

"I don't spend money
that I don't have.
I don't want money
to have power
over me."

Vanessa

When developing a financial plan with your spouse, be honest and candid about how each of you grew up viewing money. Then together create a plan for your growing family. Looking at the big picture while baby is still a baby can prevent you from hitting serious bumps later in your marriage. And don't forget: little eyes and ears will observe your habits and your child will grow up absorbing them.

For new moms who go back to work, the huge cost of child care will be a big issue. When mom stays home, it can be a tricky emotional and practical transition to drop a paycheck and gain a family member when the couple has been living a lifestyle that requires both incomes. A man may grow nervous about being the sole provider for his family. A woman may feel uneasy spending money when she isn't earning any. These are normal feelings. Guilt and worry aren't productive, so if you are experiencing these emotions, stop and think about what is generating them. If you make an effort to spend smarter, your feelings of guilt or worry should go away.

It's hard to refrain from buying your child the world when that's what you want to give him. But a four-month-old has no understanding of ownership. Give him wrapping and ribbons to play with at Christmas. Let grandparents buy a few gifts. Having willpower is so, so hard when you've envisioned your child's first holiday season in full-color daydreams with lots of presents under the tree. Soon enough children understand the concepts of quantity and even quality but not in those first couple of years. Enjoy that while you can. Give experiences. Love extravagantly. Cater to the senses. Those things don't cost much, if anything.

Couples are wise to discuss the holidays long before they arrive—whether you'll travel, what you'll spend, what you hope to be able to say about

Free Gifts
to Give Your Child

* Self-esteem
* Faith
* Patriotism
* Literacy
* Attention
* Imagination
* A servant's heart
* Creativity
* Unconditional love
* Time

"If I had stopped and thought about seven years of overlapping college, I wouldn't have bought all the baby things at six months old. Keep life Simple. Focus on your marriage. Don't be subject to your peer group. Keep the blinders on. You don't know what's really going on next door, with money or anything else."

Hillary

the season on January 2. Different expectations, often the result of different upbringings, can burst the holiday bubble for new moms and dads and lead to Grinchy arguments. Talk about it.

Then there are birthdays. I still favor going easy on presents out of common sense, being a good steward of your money, and not wanting to create a sense of entitlement in your kids. But I love to celebrate each child's unique role in our family in a big way. We take themes to extremes, but we don't spend much money. For our celebrations we've built a four-car cardboard train and a fourteen-foot space shuttle. I made a fire truck cake with my son pictured in the driver's seat. We've had a treasure-hunting, plank-walking, tattoo-wearing pirate party in which my husband stayed in costumed character for three hours. But we've never spent much on these affairs. We've proven that big fun doesn't have to mean big funds.

Looking Down

the Road

Here's a great source for objective information about Section 529 college savings plans and other ways to save and pay for college: www.savingforcollege.com. There's no investment selling or individual investment advice here but solid information, including a simple college calculator that lets you plug in your child's age and see what type of saving is necessary for higher education.

Well in advance of the big day, *before* you get swept up celebrating the milestone, decide what baby's birthday is going to mean to your family and for your finances. Then stick to your decisions and stay within the budget you set. It's easy for even a little home party to become overwhelming and expensive.

There are many ways to budget your money, and the women I interviewed offered a range of money-saving tips like buying seven hundred baby wipes at a time and shopping consignment stores. They extolled the virtues of saving for college and taking kids to the park for free. But hands down the most heartfelt financial advice moms shared was this: beware of peer pressure.

Be clear on why you're buying what you're buying, they said. Don't covet your neighbor's things or feel you have to keep up. Keep your eyes on whom you're parenting, not what they're wearing or what class they might be taking.

Take time with your husband to answer the following questions about your financial goals and your approach to spending.

Dealing with Dad
Looking Inward

1. How were my husband and I raised to think about and spend money?

2. What's most important about how we experience the holidays? Are we willing to incur debt to give gifts?

3. What were our best birthdays growing up? What made them so?

4. What should our guidelines be as we approach a big purchase?

5. Are we savers, spenders, or a combination? What would we like to change about our money habits?

6. What is being a stay-at-home mom worth to us? Or what is being a working mom worth to us?

7. What are our educational goals for our children? What will it take to achieve them?

Private Time

Intimacy after Baby

The last time I walked into a Victoria's Secret, I ran into six teenage couples passing time in the hot pink store as they waited for a table at a nearby restaurant before homecoming. They were all dressed up, giggling, and straining for some semblance of cool amid the mixed company. All I could think of was my three little boys being young men one day. I wanted to call each of those kids' moms and let her know that her precious baby was laughing at lingerie. Suddenly I felt one hundred years old.

I'd gone there to look for some pajamas, something feminine and fun, yet tasteful, to replace the fuzzy, formless, oatmeal-colored sleepwear my husband had recently told me he couldn't stand. But amid all that silky stuff, all I could think about were those kids, and my kids. Did this mean the honeymoon—on which I'd worn a different nightie every night—was truly over?

There's no doubt having children changes your sex life. Your body has been through an amazing transformation. If you're breast-feeding, your body may feel like someone else's property. A lack of sleep and an abundance of new experiences may have you feeling anything but your old self, both physically and emotionally.

Your husband may be on a very different page, eager to reconnect with you after this huge life change. But you, though also eager to reconnect, may be self-conscious about your body.

Physically, it is usually safe to resume intercourse six weeks after you deliver, as long as you feel comfortable, any stitches have healed, and your bleeding has stopped. It can take a little longer or

"One day you're a *fox;*
the next you have flab dropping
over your granny panties.
You think 'I'm ugly. I'm fat.
The baby's been pulling on me all
day.' If there's one thing I could tell
new moms it's this: **things are
not going to be *pretty*
every single day.** Marriage
is not always a home run,
a Super Bowl, a five-carat diamond.
But if my husband wants a hug,
I stop. **I hug.** When the kids were
little, there were times I thought
I was too busy.
**Don't be too busy. Your
marriage is everything."**

Hillary

less time, depending on the woman and the labor experience. After delivering a baby, vaginal dryness is a common problem but can be remedied with a lubricant. Don't be shy about asking questions or voicing concerns with your obstetrician at your six-week checkup. Discuss your options for contraception if you do not want to become pregnant again right away. It can happen, even when you're nursing.

That's as much as any pregnancy book ever told me about post-baby intimacy. I was looking for a chapter titled: "Am I Ever Going to Feel Like It Again?" Sexual desire is a private concern, but one I've come to learn many moms struggle with.

If your sex life is back on track after having a baby, congratulations and keep on! For many a mom, the months after having a baby give new meaning to the word *drained*, and sex is the furthest thing from her mind.

In general, women are more emotional than men, and men are more sexual. If anything, having a child makes a woman *more* prone to needing that emotional connection with her husband before she feels sexual. Flipping back and forth between the roles of wife and mother isn't as easy as flicking a switch. Think of people as engines. A man is often revved with a quick turn of a key, if that. A woman needs to be recharged. To refocus after a day of diapers and drool, you might need the jumper cables of conversation and hand holding to hum for a bit before feeling ready to roll.

Neither way is wrong; it's just the way most men and women are wired. Try not to retreat into yourself or draw away from your husband if you are feeling blah sexually. Discuss with honesty and respect how your urges and impulses have changed, and try to have this discussion before you're doing it in the form of a heated disagreement.

If conceiving was difficult for you, procreating—not pleasure—may have become the focus of your love life. If your pregnancy was difficult or high risk, it may feel like forever since you made love. Celebrate your new child by renewing this bond with your husband. Denise Vezey, author of *Sizzle: Seven Secrets to Reignite Your Marriage*, has advised thousands of young moms to be intentional about remembering that marriage came before motherhood.

"We put our husbands on the back burner emotionally when we have a baby. It's how God wired us, to be protective and nurturing to our kids. Most husbands understand that for a while," she writes. "But it's not just physical intimacy that they miss. They feel left out. They go from being most important to being pretty low on the list.

"I put so much into hugging my babies that I just didn't want my husband to touch me. But just because my cup is full thanks to children doesn't mean his is. That's where women grow up. You realize it's not all about you."

There needs to be a balance between looking out for your own needs and fulfilling his.

So how does mom recapture her sexual rhythm? Here are a few thoughts:

Be aware of biology. Some drugs, such as antidepressants, can dull your sex drive. Talk to your doctor if you sense that something more than adjusting to parenthood is going on with your sexual appetite. Feeling lethargic can also be caused by an improper diet. Make sure you are eating enough, getting enough calories, and staying properly hydrated, especially if you are nursing. Coffee and soda don't count!

Think sexy. What makes you feel feminine? Does exercise get your heart pumping? Does renting a romantic movie wake up your sensual side? If you want to be in the mood, you need to get in the mood. Take the initiative.

"We text message each other a lot," Tania said. "We keep fun-loving communication going during the day."

If you are full of good intentions but empty of urge and energy at the end of the day, try mornings, or invite your husband home for lunch. If you find yourself wide awake after a 3 a.m. feeding, your husband probably won't mind if you waken him. Talk it over with him. Most likely he'll be eager to figure out the best time for the two of you.

Care what you wear. It was a real wake-up call when my husband denounced my fuzzy sleepwear as completely unattractive. I really didn't think he cared what I wore to bed. But here's the thing: I was the one who didn't care. I wasn't concerned about what he thought. Be the woman you want to be. If you want to be desirable and full of desire, wear something that says so. I'm not talking garter belts and fishnet stockings, just something cute, something you feel attractive in. Your post-baby body doesn't need to be hidden head to toe. I tossed those well-worn oversized pj's away in favor of drawstring pants and a tank top, and it surprised me how much better I felt about myself. I got comfortable again in my own (stretched) skin and with a little more showing. My husband was happy too. Be proud of those curves and what they created! You are your own worst critic. Your husband will likely care more about your loving attitude than your extra pounds.

"My mother never came out in the kitchen without a robe on," Vezey shares. "Finally I know why. She wore see-through nighties every single night. She wasn't even a striking woman, really. Never talked to me about the birds and the bees, and when I got my period I was afraid to tell her. But she never, ever wore something ugly to bed. I think there's something to learn from that."

Lord knows my wardrobe has seen some serious changes since I had a baby. It's easy to get frumpy

"It's important to keep your man **happy**. He needs to make **love** to you. It's not right or wrong; it just is. It's more simple than we women make it."

Tania

when those work clothes are just not working for you anymore and you pick an outfit knowing it will likely get baby smudge on it at some point in the day. But somewhere between silk shirts and sweatpants is the hip momma you want to be. Take a little pride in your outside, and your insides will feel it.

Set a date. It may sound utterly unromantic, but many women I know put sex on the calendar.

"I remember kind of laughing when it came up in a group of women I was with, but I was intrigued. I thought, *If it works, it works*, so I talked to my husband about it," Vanessa said.

"We look at it as our day. I do little things to help me get mentally in the mood, and I don't feel like we're going straight for the goods anymore, but it makes our sex life a priority. It's a disservice to your marriage if you don't do that."

Vezey sees date setting as a positive step in making her marriage a top priority of her life: "Try to take a nap in the afternoon. Make it a priority that day. Don't just think about having sex, but truly plan your day so that you have energy for it," she said. "Have your husband put the kids to bed, so you can have a bubble bath. He may see that he can help you get in the mood by taking on more responsibility."

Think out of the box or at least the bedroom. Motherhood is quite often an exercise in losing control. On the other hand, you have the power to make your husband's day. How's *that* for control? Surprise him. It's quite possible to return to the steamy days before baby, but it just may take more effort than it used to.

One woman I know gave her husband "the look" while her kids were happily playing. Another bought some racy underwear. Still another suggested a closet encounter to her husband, whose jaw dropped open. In each case, each woman said it increased her own libido to invite spontaneity back into her marriage and initiate a rendezvous.

Your personal life is indeed personal. Some women are just much more inhibited sexually. If that's you, take baby steps toward sharing yourself more fully with your husband.

One friend confided: "When our child was three months old, I made a chocolate cake to show my husband how much I appreciated his patience with my not feeling very amorous. I think he was genuinely touched. We sat and ate the whole thing together. It didn't start out to be a romantic evening, but it was very, very memorable. Just thinking outside of myself—which is hard after you have a baby—did more than I ever imagined it could."

Touch base. When a woman's arms are quite often full of baby, she can neglect to touch her husband—to grab a shoulder, pat an arm, hold a hand. Stay connected with these small gestures, even when you are too tired or stressed out for much more. Sometimes intimacy can blossom from planting tiny seeds.

Don't give yourself grades, just grace. Adjust your idea of the perfect setting. Rose petals, champagne, and an hour's free time may need to be replaced on occasion by impromptu and quick. It's not the circumstances surrounding your sex life that matter as much as having one. Again, keep communicating. Neither of you knows what the other is thinking. One partner could be tired, but the other might perceive the lack of interest as his or her own shortcoming.

"Thirty percent of the time that we are together, I'm totally not in the mood," a close friend and mother of two told me. "But it's always, always, a good thing afterwards."

A nursing mom may find sexuality a little conflicting when a little person is often glued to her body. It's a good idea to nurse your baby shortly before you have sex, to keep your comfort level

"We have to talk about our sexual relationship more than we did before. We're like two ships passing in the night . . . but each night, my son and I greet my husband when he comes home. We're very intentional about that. Dad worked hard for us, so let's love on him. I think that says 'I still care about you. You're still important to me.' He needs respect even though you have children pulling you in another direction. I think it's something women need to remember."

Barb

and your available time at a maximum. Before baby, your breasts may have played a role in pleasure, but now they often have a utilitarian purpose. Sometimes the feeling of being owned by baby can extend to a woman's whole body.

"My kids provide a lot of fulfillment for me. I have a yearning for their smell, their touch," Tania said. "When I'm nursing, my body is being used by a baby and I feel complete. I have to remember my husband is not having this experience. He needs me, not just talking but physically. I have to be more intentional about time for him."

Several women told me they reached a nursing-era agreement with their husband that breasts were off limits for him during the months they were nursing. That helped them feel less inhibited—less protective of their bodies—during intimacy. One woman told me she simply couldn't have sex during the months she was nursing, a struggle she confided in no one at the time, and a struggle she regrets.

"It just put up a wall between us for a while," she said.

According to noted relationship researcher Dr. John Gottman, the couples he's interviewed aren't talking much about sex, and they aren't comfortable asking for what they need.

"Guys want a lot more sex than women do after a baby is born. Even three years after a baby, women's sex drive is considerably lower than men's," Gottman told CBS News. "But what the men are saying over and over again is that it's not the quantity of sex they want. They want to feel like their wives desire them. . . . That every now and then she's going to say, 'You look delicious in that blue shirt.'"

As your baby gets older, and perhaps you add to your family, intimacy can become more challenging—and more important. Privacy becomes a factor. Kids take up increasingly more time and energy, and lovemaking may land at different priority levels for a husband and wife. One man told

"I wonder if women change their view on the intimate part of a relationship when they become moms. If a midlife crisis isn't about a man's self-esteem, it's about that. All of a sudden the biological clock has done what it needed to do, and they don't need sex as much anymore. My 'clock' has nothing to do with having children. If there's no intimacy between a husband and wife, the relationship could be any other. You might as well be roommates. Talking about sex is a tough discussion, but it's one worth having if you love your spouse."

Reuben

me, "A woman can find an emotional substitute. I can't find a physical substitute."

I surely don't want my husband finding a substitute—in his real life or in his thought life. Divorce rates are frightening. On TV, adultery is entertainment. Pornography is big business. It's incumbent on a couple to talk about their needs, physical and otherwise, so they can continue to grow old *together*.

I've been known to slip in at night next to my sleeping husband, hoping he won't wake up and then snuggle up with expectations of having sex. Sometimes my sleep needs to be the priority, and other times I'm just selfish for "me" moments that are rare to find raising three children. But I have to admit that sometimes I am not interested in sex.

When my grandfather passed away, my grandmother stopped going to bed at a reasonable time. She told me it was too hard for her to be there, in their bed, alone. A much younger friend of mine

"It's not just about the *sex*.
The couple that plays together,
stays together.
Ask for help if you have to,
but make the time to
make it happen."

Brandon

died suddenly, and I think of his wife so often, knowing that she'd give anything for another night's sleep cuddled against him, for another chance to crawl in and wake him up.

We know we don't have a day to waste when it comes to our kids. The same is true of our marriage. If I were to go to sleep tonight, knowing my husband would never lie next to me again, would I rest knowing I had loved him and had honored our marriage as best I could? Would you?

Dealing with Dad
Looking Inward

1. Have my husband and I reconnected physically since I had our baby? Have I discussed with my doctor any concerns or discomfort?

2. How has our intimacy changed since we became parents?

3. Is my body image affecting my desire for romance?

4. How is sleep affecting my libido? How can I work through this?

5. What could I share with my spouse that would benefit our private time emotionally and/or physically?

Cleanup

Making Your House Work

Recently a friend of mine confided her new definition of foreplay: "My husband unloading the dishwasher and giving the kids a bath."

This can be a turn-on, indeed!

Marital researcher Gottman says his studies show that men who do more housework and child care have better sex lives and happier marriages than others. But thinking about the division of household labor may be a new concept for couples who, at one time, were home so seldom they didn't create much of a mess.

The exhaustion of parenting and procrastinating doing chores can collide overnight. If you're a

"I was a marty̆r.
I had stopped working and
knew I wasn't going back.
I always thought,
*My husband has to go to
work tomorrow, and I don't.*
So I took on too much."

Elizabeth

new stay-at-home mom, you may see housework as falling under your job description. Problem is, it keeps falling. A growing child is a growing responsibility, even without the growing laundry and baby's growing ability to slime a highchair. So if you've set yourself up as flying solo on housework, you may one day crash and burn.

Every couple has to find what works for them. Some men have been raised to believe that housework is women's work. Other couples practice a fifty-fifty split, like my friend whose husband irons his own shirts. Don't decide what your arrangement is by *not* deciding. Talk it over, with a promise that neither of you will get defensive or accusatory. Remember, you're on the same team.

My friend Erika said she felt lots of uncertainty and lacked stay-at-home-mom friends when her daughter was born. No more independence, no more contributing to the family income, and no more split chores.

"I really wanted that knight in shining armor, my husband, to come home and rescue me at the end of each day. But he wasn't always shining and receptive to the chaos he sometimes walked into. It was quite an adjustment, since I had always prided myself on being prepared and on top of things," she said.

Erika joined a Mothers of Preschoolers (MOPS) group and got some great advice and empathy for her struggles. She also woke up to the fact that she'd slipped into self-pity.

"I did have a knight in shining armor, but his job was not to save me. I needed to get up out of the ashes, so to speak, and take some control. There was no housekeeper coming, and I had no parents nearby to babysit. This beautiful baby girl was truly a gift, and my job was to enjoy her and somehow create a new family of three. I had to lower my expectations a little and realize that I was not perfect, nor was my home, nor was this lovely baby. I did not have control over everything, but thankfully God did."

Erika's ideas and philosophies on chores eventually found *her* on stage at MOPS meetings. Here are some of the ideas she shares—and her husband's take on them.

Cleaning

Lose the martyr attitude and aspirations of perfection. Ask everyone you come in contact with what works to help her manage her home. Take the ideas you like.

For Erika, it was breaking up housework into manageable pieces. One day she cleaned upstairs, one day she cleaned downstairs, one day she did bathrooms, one day she grocery shopped, and one day she prepped meals for the week.

"I had more time with my daughter because I didn't do it all at once," she said. "While she napped, I spent time doing something *I* wanted to do.

"The most important thing I learned was that my family, not my house, needed me 24-7. When it was quitting time, my husband left his office. So each night at the same time, I stopped too."

John said that picking an ending time for household work alleviated a lot of pressure on both of them. "When Erika split up the chores through the week, it was a huge benefit to our marriage, our family, her sanity, her well-being, her confidence, her energy, and our communication," John said. "We felt more peace."

Groceries

Make a complete list of everything your family consumes regularly. Erika put hers in order of her grocery store aisles. Make copies of the list and hang them on a clipboard inside your cupboard

"The biggest mistake
I made was not asking
for more help.

My husband's life didn't have

a bump in the road.

But I wanted to do it all.

I thought I could."

Julie

or pantry. Check off the item when you run out, so you're making a grocery list as you go. When you go to the store, follow your list of what you need, and you will be less prone to spontaneous buys.

Also, planning out meals ahead of time can help you avoid expensive last-minute dashes to the store. Try to plan the meals for a week and buy the ingredients you'll need all at once.

"I thought, *Great, it's her system and she'll control it*," John said. "After a few times of not getting what I wanted from the store, I learned I had to participate and add to the list. At first, I didn't like the change. But the system worked great for Erika. If she's happy, then I'm happy."

Communication

"I talked to my husband and asked, if dinner was ready when he came in the door, would he be willing to take turns cleaning up the dishes and putting the baby to bed?" Erika said. He was.

"Once we talked about it, both of us felt more settled and confident in our roles. We agreed to ask each other for help when we were overwhelmed and to keep the lines of communication open."

They also designated a spot for nonverbal communication—mail, to-do reminders, and so on. He got a small chalkboard and she bought some sticky notes.

"Erika would ask me to fix something or do something. Most of the time I didn't because of my schedule, and then I'd forget about it," John said. "She'd get frustrated that it wasn't done. I'd get frustrated because she'd keep asking when I didn't have time.

"It was great when I could finally *see* what I needed to do. If she wrote it on the chalkboard, I would get it done. Maybe not today or even tomorrow, but I would get it done. This gave her comfort, and our communication improved a lot."

"Don't expect your man to be a woman, to clean like one or to love you like one. Button your lip about how he cleans. If you keep picking on him, he will give up. He'll quit trying. His heart will get hard toward you because he can never make you happy."

Denise

At first these message areas replaced nagging. Then they became a place to leave encouragement or loving compliments for one another.

"We felt like a team again," she said.

Many couples say that making their household and marriage work after the addition of a baby means adjusting their expectations. When you've been away from the kids and the house for an evening and return to a sleeping family and the kitchen a mess and damp bath towels on the floor, you have a choice. Should you be happy that everyone is safe and happy, or frustrated the house isn't in order?

"You have to compromise," Tracy said. "When I come home, are my counters wiped off the way I would have done it? No. Are the dishes off the table? Yes. If it's not decently clean, I'm not really getting a break. And yet when you're talking about babies and kids, *clean* starts to mean something different."

"I always try to put what I'm feeling into my husband's terms," she said. "I might find a work comparison or a football analogy. I think you have to talk about it calmly, not on a night where you are huffing around cleaning up."

What does your house look like right now? At what cost? Some women seek order in their homes because much of the rest of life with children resists such consistency.

"I felt like a dog on a chain jerked all the time from one immediate need to another," says a mom of four grown children. "Keeping my physical environment neat was the one thing I had control over. I wish I could have just sat with my husband on the couch, been with my babies more.

"One day I overheard my kids in their room with a friend, and one was saying, 'You can't take the toys out of the closet and play with them or my mom will get upset!' It was a real wake-up call for me. Every strength has a weakness and every weakness has a strength."

My strength used to be weekend projects. Before having kids, my home was basically only lived in from 6 p.m. to 7 a.m. The house didn't get messy, or I wasn't around enough to see the dust. When you're home as a mom, those household projects you've been wanting to get to are in your face daily and seem more pressing. But less time is available to attack them. Some moms say they look forward to the weekends like they used to, but with less fulfillment from them. Funny how baby's schedule doesn't align itself with the big game or the pull of the Sunday paper.

"If Saturday or Sunday resembles a weekday," my friend Elizabeth says, "I'm not happy. I've learned how to make them feel different even though sometimes I'm doing the same things."

Discuss the weekend with your husband before you're in the thick of it. If possible, plan time for each of you to tackle what you need to and also have some downtime. You've been used to a weekend rhythm your entire life. Though baby's needs remain consistent, you can still make Saturdays and Sundays fun. Declare a no-cooking night and order pizza. Implement a Saturday morning family snuggle tradition. Go for donuts after church. Make it a goal to visit a different park each weekend. If you have to do laundry, do it, but fold during the football game. Give yourself a pedicure while watching a movie together.

You can still be on your toes as a parent but off your feet as a couple. Your home and housework will always be there.

Dealing with Dad
Looking Inward

1. Have my husband and I discussed divvying up some household tasks?

2. What's the chore each of us likes the most? And the least?

3. Which of Erika's ideas appeals most to us?

4. What makes a great weekend for me? For my spouse?

Looking Ahead

Who Do You Want to Be?

When you're knee-deep in diapers and show-and-tell, it's hard to imagine life after little ones. But it will come. Already I have visions of the odd reality it will be for my husband and me to sit down to dinner with only our third son remaining at home. (I don't let myself imagine them *all* gone.) I imagine looking over at Todd to share a knowing smile that says, as we often do now when we gaze at our kids, "Look what we did."

Do you have your own sign language with your husband? The high sign when it's time to leave a party? The lip biting that says to watch your tongue because little ears are listening? Years ago

Want More?

Continuing to explore the topic of marriage in the busy years of parenting is a wonderful way to honor your relationship. Here are some reading suggestions for enriching your marriage:

And Baby Makes Three: *The Six-Step Plan for Preserving Marital Intimacy and Rekindling Romance after Baby Arrives* by John M. Gottman and Julie Schwartz Gottman

Father's First Steps: *Twenty-five Things Every New Dad Should Know* by Robert W. Sears, M.D., and James M. Sears, M.D.

Childproofing Your Marriage: *Keeping Your Marriage a Priority during the Parenting Years* by Debbie L. Cherry

For Women Only: *What You Need to Know about the Inner Lives of Men* by Shaunti Feldhahn

For Men Only: *A Straightforward Guide to the Inner Lives of Women* by Shaunti and Jeff Feldhahn

The Five Love Languages: *How to Express Heartfelt Commitment to Your Mate* by Gary Chapman

the Billy Crystal movie *City Slickers* became one of our favorites. In that comedy about a trio of suburban men searching for deeper meaning at a dude ranch, the late Jack Palance plays a mysterious cowboy named Curly. As they clop along on horseback, Curly holds up a single finger to convey the meaning of life. Curly kicks the bucket in the movie, but while hilariously saving a herd of cattle, each of the friends finally understands what his "one thing," his passion, really is.

Not long after we saw that movie, my husband made me a birthday card that said "You are my Number One thing." We've held up a finger in quiet commitment ever since and signed notes that way. One year I even gave my husband his own cattle drive trip for Christmas (other years, it was socks).

There are moments when our children have had our hands so full that we didn't have the energy to lift a finger for each other. Once I heard a speaker say that in any challenging situation, you should take a step back and ask yourself, *Who do I want to be? Do I want to be a patient, forgiving mother? A generous friend? An inspiring, loyal partner?*

Marriage certainly qualifies as a challenging situation—and a glorious one. Who do *you* want to be? Make it so. Your kids are watching.

Here's hoping your marriage will long be *your* Number One thing.

Acknowledgments

From Susan

Thank you to the dozens of women who shared with me their ups and downs, moments of great triumph and great disgust, and the yearning and yelling in their hearts. You elevate the calling of motherhood by your intense love, dedication, and authenticity.

MOPS has enhanced mothering around the world and now across generations. I am confident, and deeply grateful, that its ripple effects will be felt throughout my family tree. Beth Lagerborg, thank you for asking me to dwell with you, in God's perfect timing.

Thank you to Dr. Monica Reed for reviewing this project for medical relevance and accuracy and for her dedication to women's health.

This book was possible because of women I love and was written for women I don't know, including the ones who will one day love my boys. Zach, Luke, and A.J., you are life's most amazing gifts and most humbling projects. Todd, your love inspires me. Our journey with them and with God is transforming my heart. Thank you for never giving up on my becoming a mom.

From Monica

I would like to acknowledge the team at MOPS International—Mary Beth Lagerborg, Carla Foote, and Jean Blackmer—who extended the opportunity to me to be involved in this wonderful "labor" of love; Lee Hough with Alive Communications— who continues to be an ardent supporter; and last but not least my husband, my children, and my God—all of whom make my life a wonder-filled adventure.

MOPS

A Place to Belong

My son was six months old when I attended my first Mothers of Preschoolers meeting. I knew one person in a room of 130. I was clueless about mothering and about MOPS.

Six years later, I can hardly imagine one without the other. I'm a better mother, wife, friend, leader, and Christian for the words I've heard and the women I've met. Sitting with other mothers twice a month simply elevated the calling of motherhood for me. I laughed a lot, made many friends, and deepened my understanding of the privilege and promise it is to be a mom.

MOPS began in 1973 with eight women coming together to talk, eat, share child care expenses, have a craft demonstration, and hear a short devotional. Three decades later this format lives on, with more than 100,000 women served in 4,000 groups—130 of them spread among more than 30 foreign countries. Some groups number just a handful of women; others break 100.

When it comes to creating a network of mom friends, MOPS is a no-brainer.

You might be thinking, *I'm not a joiner* or *I don't like big groups*. Here's the good news for you: MOPS breaks down big groups, and even small ones, into small tables of women who sit together for the year. They eat brunch together, discuss each speaker, plan girls' nights and park dates, celebrate life's highs, and empathize with each other's lows.

I am unabashed in my belief that MOPS changes the world by encouraging moms vocationally and spiritually as they influence the next generation. Here's my husband's opinion: "A hugely impactful thing," he says of MOPS. "I can always tell it's a MOPS Thursday because you've usually been inspired by what you've done, what you've heard, or who you've been with." (He's too private to tell you MOPS has benefited our marriage too, with all the candid speakers on relationships and intimacy.)

Stacia recognizes the same thing: "I joined for selfish reasons—time for me—and it ended up benefiting our whole family," she recalls.

For more information and to find a MOPS group close to you, check out the MOPS website at www.MOPS.org.

Susan Besze Wallace was a newspaper reporter for twelve years coast to coast, most recently with the *Denver Post*, before leaving to focus on the daily deadlines of sons Zach, Luke, and A.J. She led one of the largest MOPS (Mothers of Preschoolers) groups in the country and is a contributor to *MOMSense* magazine. Susan and husband Todd recently transplanted their busy brood to northern Virginia, where she continues writing freelance news stories and celebrating the roller coaster of motherhood in print.

Dr. Monica Reed is a physician, author, and speaker and has dedicated her life to promoting health, healing, and wellness. She currently serves as CEO of Florida Hospital Celebration Health. Dr. Reed is the author of *Creation Health Breakthrough: 8 Essentials to Revolutionize Your Health Physically, Mentally and Spiritually*. She and her husband Stanton Reed have two daughters: Melanie and Megan.

Better together...

MOPS is here to come alongside you during this season of early mothering to give you the support and resources you need to be a great mom.

Get connected today!

Mothers of Preschoolers

2370 S. Trenton Way, Denver CO 80231
888.910.MOPS • www.MOPS.org/bettermoms

Perfect Gifts for a New Mom!

New moms run into a host of new challenges once baby arrives. *The New Mom's Guides* go straight to the heart of these matters, offering moms guidance and encouragement in this new season of life.